The King Gets Fit

Story by Allen Saddler
Pictures by Joe Wright

Oxford University Press

Oxford University Press, Walton Street, Oxford OX2 6DP
Oxford   New York   Toronto
Delhi   Bombay   Calcutta   Madras   Karachi
Petaling Jaya   Singapore   Hong Kong   Tokyo
Nairobi   Dar es Salaam   Cape Town
Melbourne   Auckland

and associated companies in
Berlin   Ibadan

Oxford is a trade mark of Oxford University Press
© text copyright Allen Saddler
© artwork copyright Joe Wright
This edition first published for Oxford Reading Tree 1991

ISBN 0 19 916402 9

Printed in Hong Kong

One day some acrobats came to perform on the Palace Green. They did somersaults and cartwheels and walked on their hands, upside down. They screwed themselves up into little balls and they stood on each other's heads. The King was delighted.

That night he tried to do a cartwheel in his bedroom, but he bumped into a chair and fell over with a crash.

'Oh!' said the King. 'It's not so easy as it looks.'

'You'll hurt yourself,' said the Queen.

'I have,' said the King. 'Can I stand on your head?'
The Queen went into her bedroom and locked the door.

The next morning the King climbed on to the mantelpiece and jumped off with another crash.
The breakfast jumped off the table.

'What are you doing?' said the Queen.

'I'm trying to be an acrobat,' said the King.

'You'll be an accident,' said the Queen, 'if you're not more careful.'

After breakfast the King put on his shorts and ran up the passage. Then he ran back again.

'Whatever are you doing now?' said the Queen.

'I have to get fit to be an acrobat,' said the King, as he rushed past. He hopped up the steps on one foot and hopped down on the other. 'Makes your ankles strong,' he explained.

That night the King went to bed early.

'Early to bed and early to rise,' he said, 'makes a man wise and healthy.'

'You've got it wrong,' said the Queen. 'It's wealthy and wise and healthy.'

But the King didn't rise early. He slept very late. When he woke up he said,

'Oh dear. I'm stiff all over. I don't feel well. I think I'll stay in bed for a bit.'

The maid came to make the bed.

'Leave it for today,' said the King. 'I'm still in it.'

'Well, you'll have to get out of it then,' said the maid.

'My legs are sore,' said the King, 'and my back aches. You'd better get the Royal Doctor.'

The Royal Doctor examined the King from head to toe.

'You need more exercise,' he said. 'You muscles are weak.'

'I know,' said the King. 'I'd better stay here and rest them.'

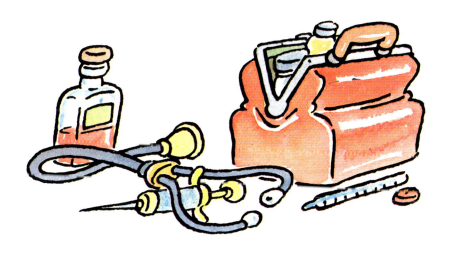

'No you don't,' said the Royal Doctor. 'You need to run up and down the passage.'

'I did that yesterday,' said the King, 'and look at me now.'

So the King put his shorts on
and hobbled up the passage
saying, 'Oh dear, my poor legs.'

'Why don't you sit down then?'
said the Queen.

'Because it hurts my back,' said
the King, 'that's why.'

The Royal Doctor said that the King must drink a lot of beef tea.

'I don't like that stuff,' said the King.

'All the better,' said the Queen. 'It will do you more good.'

'I don't see that,' said the King.

'You never see anything,' said the Queen.

After he had drunk two cups of beef tea the King felt sick.

'I don't think I want to be an acrobat after all,' he said.

He went back to bed and played noughts and crosses with the Court Jester, who always let the King win.

The Royal Doctor came in often, and looked at the King's tongue.

'Have you ever tried hopping on one leg?' he said.

'Yes,' said the King, miserably. 'It hurts my ankles.'

The Court Jester kept telling the
King funny stories, but the King
didn't laugh. The Court Jester got
upset and started to cry.

'It's not much fun if you don't
laugh,' he said.

'I'm sorry,' said the King, 'but I don't
feel like laughing with backache.'

The next day the King felt a bit better.

'I think I might take a little walk today,' he said. 'But slowly, mind.'

He walked with the Queen out to the Palace Green. The King fed the ducks in the pond and started to chase a squirrel, but soon stopped.

'Oh!' said the King, 'my legs still hurt like pins and needles.'
'You are a baby,' said the Queen. 'Would you like to see the acrobats?'
'No,' said the King. 'I wouldn't.'